Ben's Bike

Written by Jill Eggleton

Illustrated by Chantal Stewart

The people in the book

Ben

Grandpa

Mum

The park
in the book

Ben went to the park. He saw all the kids riding bikes.

They went in and out of the mud…

SWOOSH!

SWOOSH!

They got mud all over them.

"I wish I had a bike," said Ben.

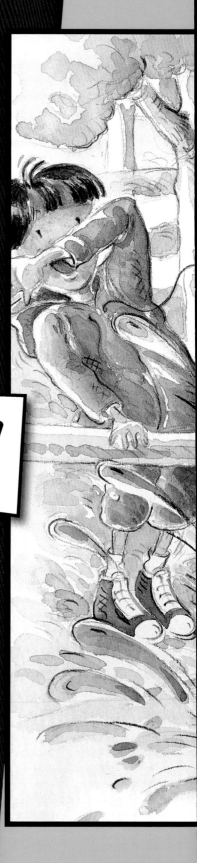

A big kid came up to Ben.

"Where's your bike?" she said.

"I haven't got a bike," said Ben.

"You have to get a bike," said the big kid.
"All the kids have bikes."

The big kid went off fast.
Mud went up...

SWOOSH!

Ben is...?

At home, Ben said,

"I wish I had a bike.
All the kids have bikes.
Please can I have a bike
that can go in the mud?"

Ben's mum looked sad.

"We can't get you a bike,"
she said.
"We have no money for bikes."

How can
Ben get a
bike?

Ben's grandpa came to stay.
He sat down with Ben.
They saw kids on bikes.

"I wish I had a bike," said Ben,
"but I can't have one.
We have no money for bikes."

Ben's grandpa went to the bike shop.

He got...
wheels
handlebars
pedals
a chain

He got...
a seat
a horn
a bell

Then he went into the shed.

"You can't come in," he said to Ben.

Ben can't go in the shed.
He will...

see the bike?

laugh at
Grandpa?

Ben's grandpa was in the shed all week. Then, on Saturday, he went to get Ben.

"Come with me," he said.

He put his hands over Ben's eyes and he opened the shed door.

"Now you can look," he said.

"WOW," said Ben.
"What a **cool bike!**"

Ben is...?

Ben took his bike to the park.

The big kid came up to Ben.

"That's a cool bike," she said.
"Can it go in the mud?"

"It can," said Ben.

Ben will...

go in the mud?

go home?

Ben got on his bike and rode off fast—**very** fast! Mud went up...

SWOOSH!

"**Wow**," said all the kids. "Look at Ben on that cool bike!"

The End

Labels

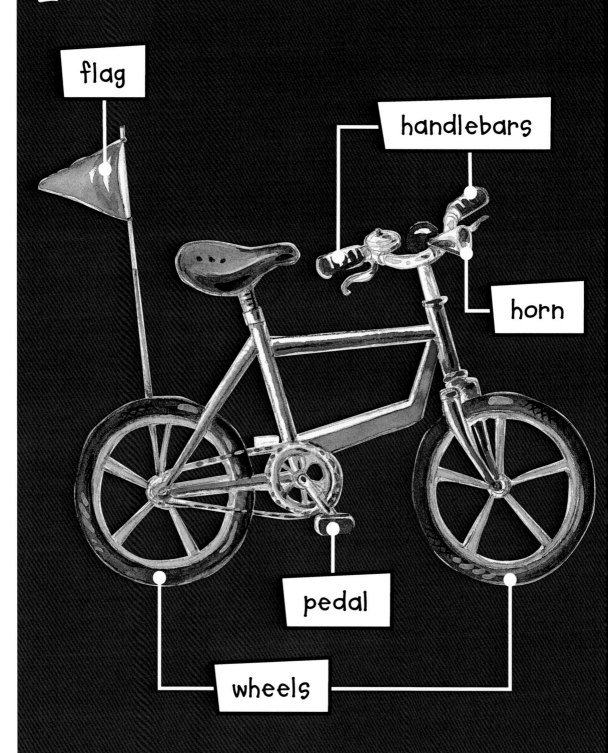

Which labels are right?

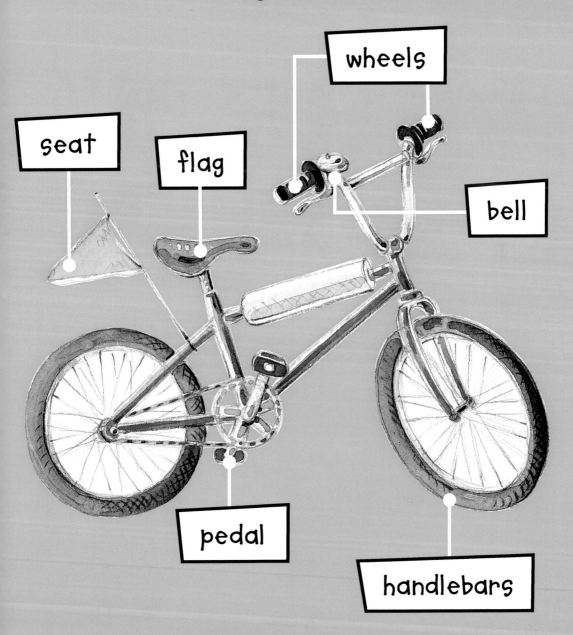

seat

flag

wheels

bell

pedal

handlebars

Word Bank

bell

bike

chain

handlebars

horn

mud

pedals

seat

shed

wheels